LITTLE STONE
AND THE STAR

Copyright © Bee Ifezue 2019.
All rights reserved.
First paperback edition printed 2015 in the
United Kingdom
A catalogue record for this book is available from
the British Library.
ISBN 978-0-9934611-1-8
No part of this book shall be reproduced or transmitted in
any form or by any means,
electronic or mechanical, including photocopying,
recording, or by any information retrieval
system without written permission of the publisher.
Published by Scribblecity Publications
Printed in Great Britain
Although every precaution has been taken in the
preparation of this book, the publisher and
author assume no responsibility for errors or omissions.
Neither is any liability assumed for
damages resulting from the use of this information
contained herein.

Dedicated to Kene

A Day Out

One day Little Stone and his grandma went to visit grandma's friend, granny Granite who lived by the side of the field

which overlooked an old wooden hut.

He made friends with Fin and Din her two energetic grandchildren who were holidaying with her.

The first night as he lay beside his grandma, they both gazed up into the sky dotted with shiny stars which twinkled magically in the velvet dark sky.

Grandma and Little Stone chuckled as the twinkly stars seemed to give them playful winks.

"That is **Orion**," she said, "Such a shiny group of stars. Over there is **Great Bear** and beside it is the **Little Bear**," she continued.

"Look at that bright pointed star Grandma, what is it called?' Asked Little Stone as he gazed at the enormous silver star glistening amongst the lesser stars.

"Ah, that is a special star. It is the **Guardian** star." Said the old stone. "Whenever time you're lost, follow it and it will lead you home."

Little Stone smiled sleepily at the beautiful stars and for a brief second he thought the

guardian star gave him a friendly wave.

As he slept, he dreamt of mother bears and baby bears.

The Twins

The next day, the sun shone brightly and the morning dew shimmered like rainbow pebbles in the sunlight. The bees raced to scoop the fresh dew from the open flowers while the birds chirped merrily in the nearby trees.

It was a beautiful morning and as Little Stone pondered on what to do for the day, he heard laughter coming from the fields.

Little Stone wondered who that could be as the loud shouts grew nearer.

Suddenly Fin and Din tumbled up to him from the field quite energetically.

The twins were quite happy to see the little stone, and both spoke excitedly.

"Hello Little Stone, **come and play** with us!" Din shouted loudly as he jumped up and down.

Little Stone stared at Din curiously wondering how he got the nasty crack on his head.

"**Yes, let's go!**" roared an excited Fin as he lept in the air.

The twins twirled and skipped, laughed and squealed. They were full of beans and just wouldn't stay still.

What an excitable pair thought an amused Little Stone.

The twins leaped and hopped like two impatient grasshoppers,

"Race you down to the bottom of the field!" Din shouted.

Before Little Stone could blink, the twins **zoomed** down the field and disappeared into the long green blades of grass.

Little Stone didn't want to be left behind.

"**Wait** for me!" He called as he quickly scurried after Fin and Din as fast as he could.

The Race

The three stones raced into the field.

A grumpy fluffy white sheep grazing in the grass bleated angrily.

"**Baa, baa**, don't get into my hooves! It hurt the last time you got stuck in it. You **baa-ad, baa-ad** boys." She scolded.

"Sorry!" yelled the twins as they rolled swiftly by. The mother sheep shook her head and carried on chewing the fresh juicy grass.

Little Stone smiled shyly at the mother sheep as he carefully scurried past her.

After a little while, they arrived at the end foot of a mound.

"Let's go see what is on the other side of that hill," said Din.

"Isn't that going a bit too far from our field?" Asked Fin.

Din stopped and picked a red flower and placed it near the side of the path.

"There, now we will find our way home from here" he said.

Little Stone and Fin both agreed that it was a great idea.

With the red flower firmly and safely tucked between the grass, the three small stones wandered off to explore the other side of the hill.

The Lost Stones

As the sun set, the tired stones had had enough of playing and decided to make their way home. They rolled to the side of the hill and stopped by the bend where they had placed the red flower; however, to their horror, the flower had vanished.

"**Oh no!** The sheep must have eaten it," shrieked Fin in horror.

The three stones were now lost and hadn't the slightest clue where they were.

As night fell, the stones began to get very worried.

"I am sure it's that way." stammered Fin, wishing it wasn't so dark.

"No, I think it's the other way," Din whimpered quietly.

If only I wasn't so curious thought Little Stone to himself.

"**Errm**, maybe we should wait here until morning. We'd be able to see a lot better when it's daylight," suggested Fin, and they all nodded in agreement.

Like popcorn, the stars began to pop out of the sky and the three stones lay close together waiting for sunrise.

All of a sudden, a loud ghostly noise floated from above the tall trees.

"**Aaaah!**" the three stones screamed. An owl fluttered above them.

"**TuWOO! TuWOO!** Sorry to have frightened you, but shouldn't you three be at home?" He hooted as he flew past.

The three stones sighed in relief. It wasn't a horrible monster after all.

After a long dreadful moment of silence, Little Stone began to jump up and down in excitement.

"I know the way! I know the way!" He jumped excitedly, as he pointed to sky. "It is over that way."

The twins exchanged puzzled glances at each other.

"The sky?" Fin asked.

"No!" chuckled the little stone. "The **guardian** star is the big star by the right. Grandma said whenever you are lost, follow it and it will lead you home." he said.

The Star

"Alright, what are we waiting for?" Cheered Din. "**Let's go!**"

The three stones headed off in high spirits, following the star.

Along the way, they came across some ants carrying large berries.

"Where are you kids going this late?" Asked the ants curiously.

"We got lost... but now we are going home. All we have to do is follow the star, see?" Replied Little Stone.

"Really? Where do you live?" Asked the concerned ants.

"Near the edge of the field by the old wooden hut." Answered Little Stone

"O dear!" Exclaimed the ants. "You are heading in the wrong direction".

"We will show you the way, come along," called the ants as they scurried off.

Fin and Din happily accepted the ants' offer. Little stone peered up at the twinkling star through his large round glasses. The star appeared even bigger and brighter than ever.

"**Come on** Little Stone, hurry up!" Called Fin and Din.

Little Stone shook his head sadly as he rememebered what grandma had said.

"No!" He replied "I am going that way."

"Do what you want," shrugged Din. Then he and Fin quickly scampered after the ants.

Little Stone watched them roll into the distance. He glanced around him, a bit scared as the night critters chirped loudly.

He looked up at the sky and there was the **star** shining comfortingly down at him.

Follow The Star

A Little Stone set off on his journey back home, all of a sudden a dark shadow cast over him.

"Where are you going?" a gruff voice demanded.

Little Stone shivered with fright. He peered into the dark and there in front of him was a grasshopper and a caterpillar.

"I am Sorry, I hope we didn't frighten you?" apologised the grasshopper as he coughed to clear his throat.

"This is my friend, Caterpillar, he doesn't speak very much." The caterpillar **shook** his head in reply.

"Tell me, what is a little stone like you wandering by yourself at a time like this?" Asked the grasshopper.

"The star is guiding me home," Little Stone replied.

"Would you like some company?" offered the grasshopper.

"**Yes!** I would like that," replied the little stone happily.

"We met some sheep and horses with their owners and they were also heading this way." Said the grasshopper.

Little Stone enjoyed their company and thought it very kind of them to accompany him. The chatty grasshopper narrated how they had been woken by a **bright** light

and lots of **noise**, and now they wanted to go somewhere else to find some peace and quiet for the night.

After a while of following the star, Little Stone blinked as he squinted ahead of him. Somewhere in the distance was a **huge** dark shape, and in front of it were a group of animals.

"These are the sheep and horses I met earlier," said the grasshopper.

Little Stone could see the angry mother sheep he had met earlier and her lamb. He wandered what the animals were looking at.

Home at Last

"**W**here have you been?" Asked a gentle voice beside him.

"**Grandma!**" Shouted Little Stone. "I am so glad to see you! What are you doing here?" He asked excitedly.

"This is where we live, dear." Grandma replied a bit puzzled.

"**Yes!** It worked! It worked!" Exclaimed Little Stone quite overjoyed.

He excitedly told Grandma about his adventure and how he had followed the star.

Later that night, Little Stone bid the grasshopper and the caterpillar goodnight. He was happy they had found a quiet spot by the edge of the hut.

It was a silent night and all was calm. All the animals lay quietly by the old hut.

The twins were not yet back, and their grandmother wasn't worried. She knew they would be home by daylight.

That night, Little Stone lay cosily beside his grandma. He could see the inside of the hut a lot more clearly now that everyone had gone.

Inside the hut, he could see a human baby peacefully sleeping in a cradle. There was something particularly special about the night, and something even more special about this baby.

As the star **twinkled** brightly above the old wooden hut, Little Stone drifted into a sweet sleep. Somewhere in the distance he could hear an amazing sound of many voices singing. "**Glory to God** in the highest and on earth peace..."

www.ingramcontent.com/pod-product-compliance
Lightning Source LLC
LaVergne TN
LVHW051227070526
838200LV00057B/4634